ROBERT BOUNDY

FOUNDATIONS

A WORKBOOK TO DEVELOP PRACTICE SKILLS AND KNOWLEDGE FOR PLAYING THE DRUM KIT.

FEATURING:

14 KEY METHODS // TECHNICAL EXERCISES // PLAYALONG

CHARTS // DRUM KIT CONCEPTS // ONLINE LESSONS

Table of Contents

Hello there,

Welcome to my book, *Foundations – Practice skills and knowledge for playing the Drum Kit*, created by Rob's Drum Shed Productions.

It is my pleasure to present you with a book filled with concepts, exercises, and play along charts that were written to help my students develop a good, regular practice routine.

My intention is to help reinforce what you learn in your lessons by presenting a variety of materials that I have written and arranged over the years. You can explore this to a greater extent through my website: **https://www.robsdrumshed.com.**

Students can supplement the lessons in this book by registering on the website, all you have to do is go to the resources section, click on enquiry at top of the page, and fill in the details – be sure to write *Foundations* in the message section. I will send you a password by return email.

The resources section contains .pdf files, play alongs, and some demonstration clips of the different lessons available.

Most of the content here is original material. Well, it's my reworked version or interpretation of experiences and lessons that have helped me become a better player. It begins with my documentation of 14 Key Methods from Gene Krupa's *Drum Method*, first published in 1938. I began playing drums in 1968 at The Adelaide College of Music, and have practiced and developed these methods by performing in bands and ensembles, working on my skills, and becoming a "working" musician in 1982, eventually performing in both Australia and The United States. I have worked in retail music stores since 1985, all of which has supported my learning, research, study, and performance of original music.

In 2018, I graduated from The University of Adelaide with an Honours Degree – Bachelor of Music (Music Education and Pedagogy) with First Class Honours.

I have been often asked at gigs by other drummers to explain my ideas. How I acquired this knowledge and what I learned from it can be described as "Constructivism". The learning theory is explained as "using experiences to construct knowledge and meaning to form ideas and concepts". I'm continually documenting my experiences through formal lessons, studies, practice, or performances, and compiling what I learn in journal notes and written musical notation. I also make sure to relisten to audio recordings and rewatch video footage of practices and live performances. All of this has helped to improve my skills as a performer and a teacher. I have used all these tools (and then some) to compile this book and develop it into a structured learning sequence. I myself use the elements of this book on a daily basis, and in 2005 when I began to teach in the Private School Education system, I formalised the concepts for my students to have a solid foundation to rely on.

Throughout my working life, I have come into contact with the most amazing and creative human beings, drummers/musicians/teachers, and businesspeople almost on a daily basis. It has fuelled my passion for the instrument, and made critical thinking and self-analysis a daily habit, constantly motivating and inspiring me.

I am grateful for all these experiences: they keep me on the path of this musical journey.

Enjoy,

The Method

The lessons presented here are based on the format from my first drum tutor book, Gene Krupa's Drum Method. We will follow the sequence of instruction as Krupa recommends – it is of equal importance to the content. I must add that I have slightly altered the sequence from my own experience to help with the continuity of the material.

The content is based upon Tom Jackson's The Complete Drummers Guide, though I have spiced it up a little, making it more personal and student centred for my private drum set students.

In 'Level 1: Foundations', there are six modules that begin to explore the format of Krupa's key methods. The detail gradually becomes more refined as you go through the stages of learning presented in these lessons – and some lessons contain more than one part.

The methods are then reinforced when you progress to the next two levels.

The online lesson sheets available through the website are presented as .pdf files, which I highly recommend that you print out. This way, you can have a hard copy to keep in a folder so that you can edit or make notes on (in pencil) to reference when you need.

I would advise that you also maintain a practice diary and keep a log of your lessons each week as this assists in tracking your progress.

All these books are available from the RDS website (https://www.robsdrumshed.com) on the resources page.

The next section of this book is Level 2: Intermediate syllabus. This section takes the student through more advanced lessons and song transcriptions.

The Beginning of the Foundation

Gene Krupa's Drum Method (Interpreted by Robert Boundy)

Gene Krupa's Drum Method follows a format that is divided into fourteen key methods, which will be discussed in detail in the following text. The introduction states that:

'Music belongs to the order of principles capable of charging the atmosphere with power. By dividing the three-fold root of MUSIC we get Melody, Harmony and Rhythm. The purpose this book hopes to serve, will be a scientific approach to the dynamic field of Rhythm through the study of drumming'.[1]

In any area of learning, the sequence of instruction is of equal importance to the content. The beginning foundation is laid for effective drum set instruction, set out in the following sequence in Krupa's Drum Method: beginning with a focus on the snare drum, exquisitely put in Krupa's own words: "The Snare Drum, by virtue of its importance, will be studied first".[2] Each of the **fourteen stages** of learning will be as follows:

1. **The First Key method** is the selection of a correct practice pad, so that beginners don't begin their development depending on the drum for rebound. Position and form are the first requisites of rudimental drumming.

2. **The Second Key method** gives specific reference to the importance of selecting appropriate pairs of drumsticks. The important things are tone, weight, straightness, and selecting a size of the model that most suits the individual.

3. **The Third Key method** covers hand technique and stick grip, how to hold the sticks, and explains the different grips, both traditional and matched grip.

4. **The Fourth Key method** covers the rudiments of music: relative value of notes and rests, and comparative table of relative note values, the table of time, dotted notes, triplets and artificial note groups; and the symbols: staff, clefs, measures and bars, the repeat signs, dynamics, time and tempo marks.

5. **The Fifth Key method** is reading exercises – incorporating note groups and technical skills to execute these groupings using the downstroke and the upstroke. Ted Reed went on to expand on this concept in 1958 with the release of *Progressive Steps to Syncopation for The Modern Drummer*, created exclusively to address syncopation.[3] The text is somewhat dated, and modern music teaching methods are now deemed as more effective.

   When presented as-written, this can be arguably uninspiring, un-motivating, and one dimensional for the learning student. Much of the focus is on teaching skills, and teachers develop many of their own examples from it.

---

[1] Gene Krupa, Introduction. *Drum Method* (New York, Robbins Music Corporation, 1938)

[2] Krupa, 37

[3] Ted Reed, *Progressive Steps to Syncopation for the Modern Drummer*. (Florida, Ted Reed Publications, 1958)

6. **The Sixth Key method** covers the practical application of different groups of sticking that is referred to as drum rudiments – single stroke rolls, double stroke rolls, paradiddles and their variations, roll studies, and working at a suggested tempo of 140 beats per minute. The roll chart begins from the three-stroke ruff, five-stroke roll through to the 15-stroke roll, triplet rolls, cut time applications of rolls with eighth note hand movements. Even number rolls, drag paradiddles, single and double drags, single stroke rolls incorporating the single stroke ruffs, compound beats, ruff paradiddles, paratriplets, and flams: flamacues, flam tap, flam accent no 2, flamadiddles, double flamadiddles, triple flamadiddles, and lesson 25.

7. **The Seventh Key method** present us with performance pieces for snare drum: "The Downfall of Paris",[4] a 2/4 march time 48 bar solo arranged in 4 parts, incorporating the rudiments with sticking written in for clarity and accuracy of performance; "The Breakfast Call" a cut time, US Army Field Music Service Call from the Civil War;[5] "The Three Camps", a comprehensive, 28 bar roll study in 12/8 compound time;[6] and "Dinner Call",[7] the final piece in 6/8 compound time 20 bar solo, also from the rich history of American Rudimental military drum solos.

8. **The Eighth Key method** is study of the bass drum. It is extremely important in contemporary music, and a great deal of time needs to be spent on exercises to improve the coordination of hands and feet. Current teaching methods have embraced Gene's philosophy in regard to seat height, leg and ankle freedom, and relaxation. Krupa's technical insight explains the need to be careful not to allow the beater ball to remain against the head after the beat – try to pick the beats off the drum, giving you a sharp, clean boom and greatly improving your speed.

Marvin Dahlgren and Elliot Fine from the University of Minnesota wrote in the 4-Way Coordination book, explaining the development of coordination between both hands and feet.

The development of this technique will lead to complete independence.[8] Krupa stated that many drummers neglected to practise as much on their bass drum because of the disturbance caused by the loud sound of the drum. This could explain the Dahlgren's reference to the feet playing a subordinate part in a drummer's development. Krupa suggests that this can be easily overcome by getting a pedal practice pad – a forerunner to today's modern electronic drum kits and their popularity with new students and families that can suffer from the disturbance of a drummer's daily practice.

After the first stage of development, the second stage of student development is the drum kit: incorporating bass drum/s, Hi-hat, crash and ride cymbals, and tom toms. We continue with the next group of key methods.

---

[4] Rollo Laylan, *The Downfall of Paris*, accessed August 22nd 2017 http://vicfirth.com/ancient-rudimental-solo-downfall-of-paris
[5] Rollo Laylan, Field of Music US Army/Service Call ,*The Breakfast Call* accessed August 22nd 2017 https://www.youtube.com/watch?v=NGAockidzRs
[6] Rollo Laylan, *Three Camps*, Accessed August 22nd 2017, https://www.youtube.com/watch?v=NgWfkbvbRt8
[7] Rollo Laylan, *Dinner Call* Accessed August 22nd 2017, https://www.youtube.com/watch?v=8I6YGO65ACU
[8] Marvin Dahlgren and Elliot Fine, *4-Way Coordination* (New York, 1963)

9. **The Ninth Key method** is the study of the foot cymbals or the Hi-hat, played with the left foot. They were originally intended for the after beat for the offbeat cymbal effect. Krupa suggest that you select two eleven-inch (1938 standards) Avedis Zildjian cymbals for your all-around work, selecting one cymbal that is a little heavier for underneath and lower in pitch, and discouraging the use of cymbals with a strong fundamental bell tone. Instead, choose cymbals that are rich in harmonic overtones that splash instead of ring. The procedure for mounting the cymbals is then explained in exquisite detail, teaching the learner much needed skills in the importance of care and maintenance of this paramount section of the drum set. The development of the left foot in good Hi-hat work suggests learning to work your left foot alone before trying to combine it with the right foot bass drum practice. Once you have mastered the use of the left foot for opening and closing the Hi-hat, then proceed on to the use of both feet. The practice explanation given states: when the right foot, (bass drum) goes down the left foot (Hi-hat) comes up, and when the left goes down the right comes up, an alternating foot movement like the single strokes on the snare drum. The height is indicated that an inch to an inch-and-a-half opening between the cymbals gives the best results. This is at a recommended tempo of 110 beats per minute.

10. **The Tenth Key method** involves playing the Hi-hat with sticks incorporating what is now the whole drum kit. It introduces the rudiments: four-stroke ruff on the Hi-hat, and both feet using bass drum and open Hi-hat. The concept of building on the foundational work set on the previous page uses the previous foot exercises combined with the four-stroke ruff and the next rudiment the seven-stroke roll.

11. **The Eleventh Key method** is cymbals and cymbal playing. The recommendation is for four cymbals of different tones. Today, standard setup for the learner drummer still consists of this combination, e.g. a 20" ride cymbal, 14" Hi-hats, 16" crash and 18" crash. This gives a student the chance to develop right and left hand coordination as introduced in Jackson's The Complete Drummers Guide, in adapting the accented 16th notes as drum set fills exercises.[10] This progressive structured learning is again reinforced by Krupa's original insights and combined in the popular methods of today.

---

[9] Gene Krupa, 57

[10] Tom Jackson, *The Complete Drummers Guide* (Melbourne, DTB Concepts 2012) 33

12. **The Twelfth Key method** is playing with brushes, introducing the student to the art of playing swish or legato strokes. The first set of brush rudiments is then explained as the tap down and up, and swish stroke. The concept of playing the right hand on the Egyptian or 'Greeko'[11] cymbal introduces the student to the beginnings of what is now referred to as ride cymbal playing: the right hand plays the repetitive ostinato patterns, holding the drum kit patterns together and supporting the ensemble, setting a solid, rhythmic foundation.

13. **The Thirteenth Key method** is the rim shot, defining accents and non-accents. Dynamics are introduced and technical execution becomes more refined. Technology plays an important part with visual aids to help the student develop accuracy with stick control and stick heights. George Lawrence Stone, author of the bestselling method: *Stick Control*, released the next book: *Accents and Rebounds*, an advanced textbook designed to follow and reinforce student control and dynamic execution. Stone states that it is presented at the solicitation of many leading instructors, who, having used the former book with such gratifying results, asked for material to follow in their daily workout. The drums, from their very nature, possess potential for accentuation far greater than any other musical instrument. Hence the drummer is looked to above all other for the utmost in dynamics.[12] Krupa's method once again presents the dependable teaching strategy to be followed.

14. **The Fourteenth Key method** and final stage for student development is playing along to music. A great deal of practical knowledge can be gained by playing along with music presented with arrangements and scores. In this stage of development, they are to be used as a guide to improve aural skills. The introduction of studying and transcribing scores and charts is the next step in the process of education and music appreciation for the student.

---

[11] Gene Krupa, 69

[12] George Lawrence Stone, *Accents and Rebounds,* (Massachusetts, George B Stone & Son, Inc. 1961) 3

Module One

Elements

Lesson 1: Technique – The Foundation

General Technique/ Grip (Krupa's Third Key method)

The technique we recommend for the hands is a relaxed, natural grip. This is essential for effective drumming. There are three main grips used in modern playing. Many players use the matched grip (Germanic) style, in which you play with the sticks held the same way in both hands, palms facing down. It is the most versatile of the percussion stick/mallet grips. This grip is described in detail below. There is another version of the matched grip called the French grip, which was developed mainly for playing fast and relaxed single stroke rolls on timpani. It is also used by many top drum set players such as Carter Beauford, Billy Cobham, and Simon Phillips, and involves a slight rotation of the hand so that the thumbnail faces upward (the palms face toward each other). The French grip can be learned later, since it builds on the principles of the Germanic grip. Also used for the drum set is the traditional grip, in which the left hand cradles the stick in the style of marching band snare drummers. Players such as Virgil Donati, Thomas Lang, Buddy Rich, Tony Williams, Steve Gadd, and Max Roach, as well as many other great players, use this grip.

Matched Grip (Germanic):

1. Hold the stick with the fulcrum (grip/balance point) between the flat part of your thumb and first joint of your index finger (Fig. 1). The fulcrum is the pivot point on a lever (in our case, the pivot point of our drumstick). Imagine there is a pin going through the centre of the thumbnail and emerging through the first knuckle of the index finger. This is the basis of the Control Grip (see fig. 3 below).

2. Let the butt of the stick rest on the soft part of the palm at your hand below your pinky-finger, just above the wrist (Fig. 2). This part of the hand is referred to as the "shock absorber" since it acts as a pad to absorb the energy of the rebounding stick.

3. Wrap your third, fourth, and fifth fingers loosely around the stick and do not squeeze. Do not close the space between your thumb and index finger and keep only the first knuckle of the index finger on the stick. This is called the Control Grip (Fig. 3) and it is the starting point from which you will learn the techniques in these lessons.

Note that it is also possible to close the space between the thumb and fingers and drop the second knuckle of the index finger onto the stick. This is called the Power Grip (Fig.4) and is used for harder playing (medium to loud) and same faster figures utilising open double strokes. Marching and rudimental players and corps often use the power grip.

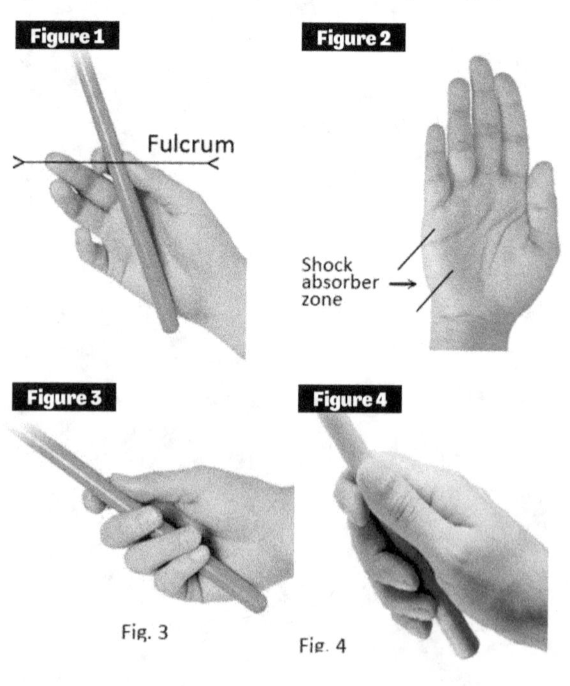

Lesson 2: Symbolism

The Rudiments of music (Krupa's Fourth Key method)

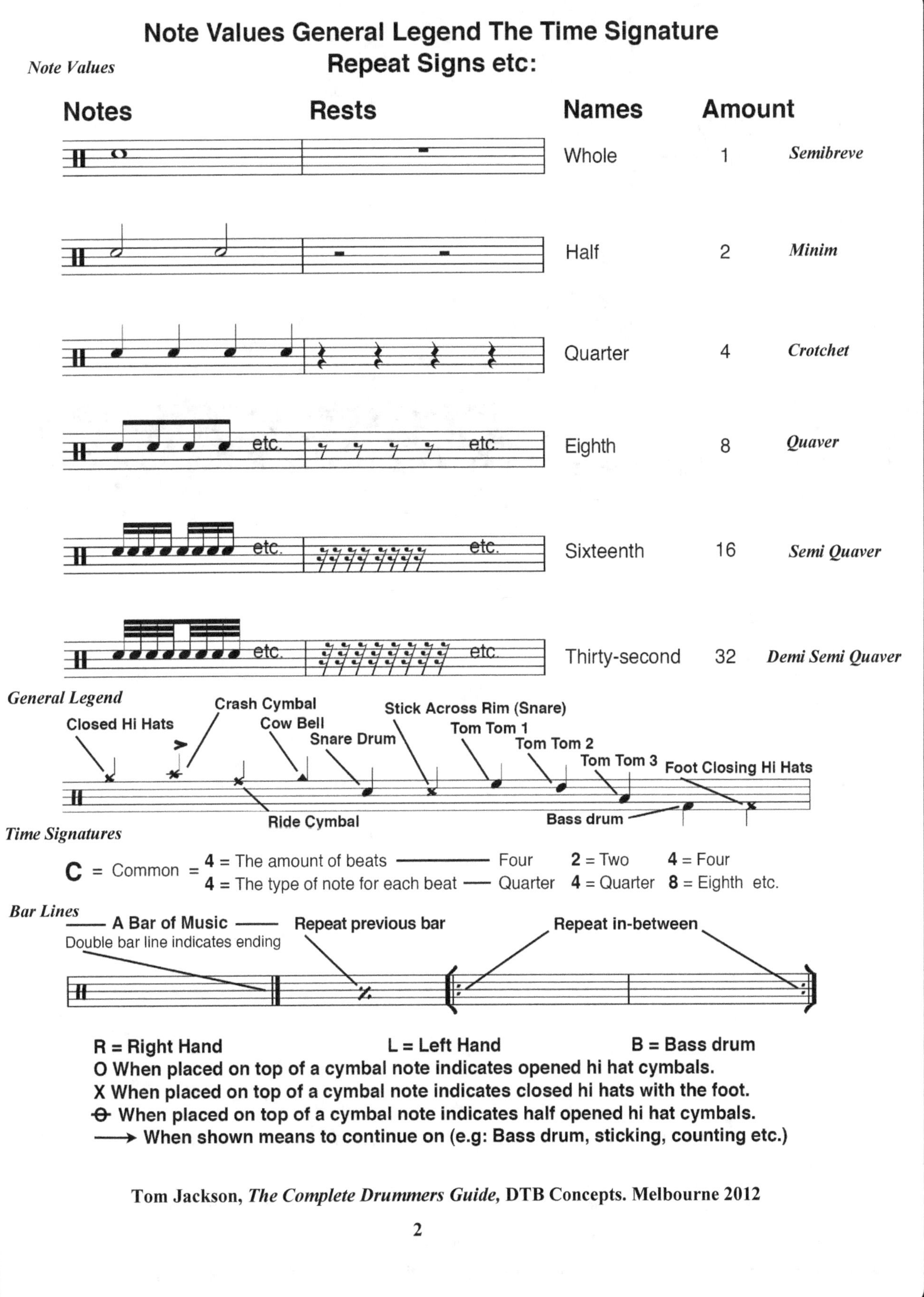

Tom Jackson, *The Complete Drummers Guide*, DTB Concepts. Melbourne 2012

2

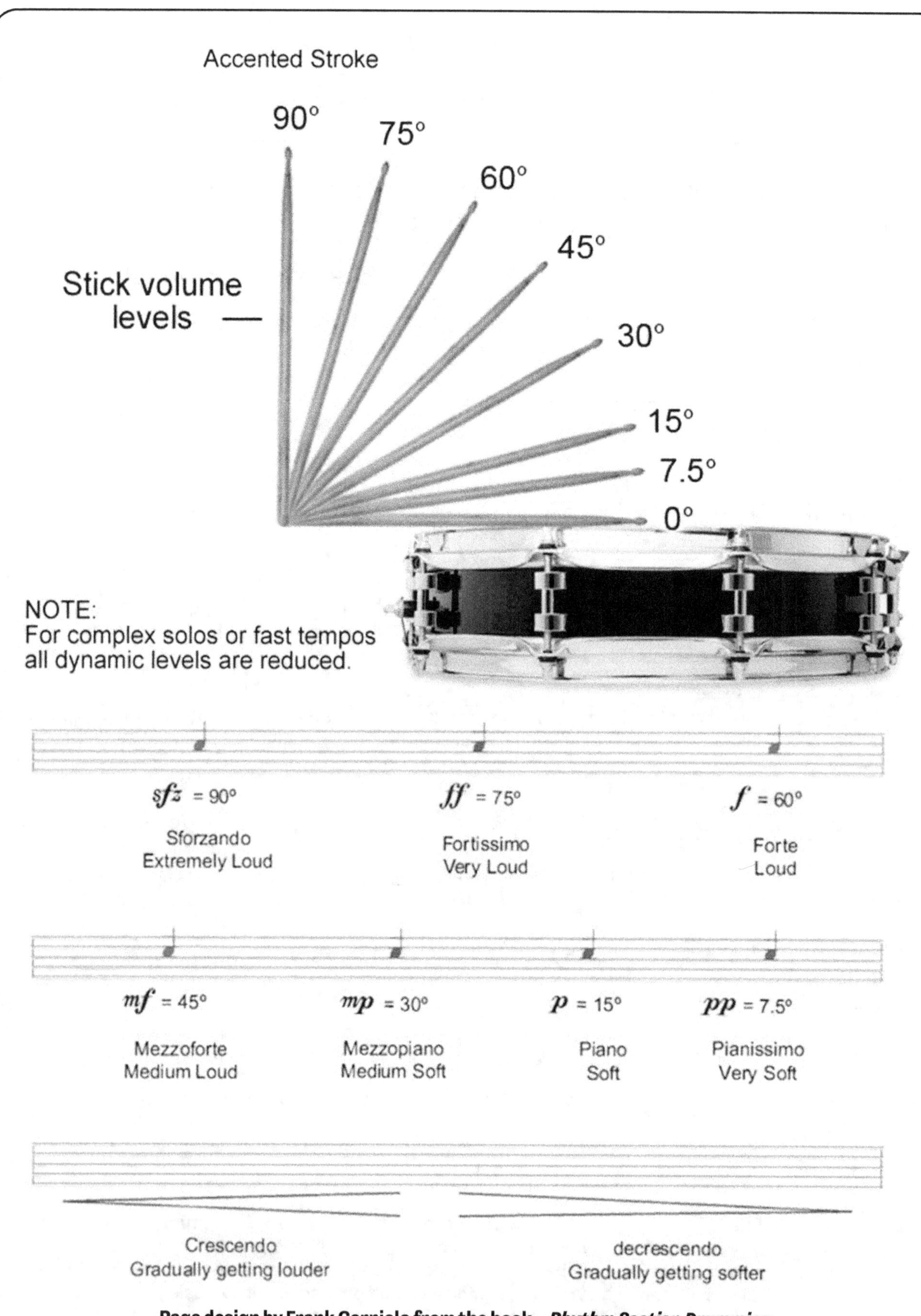

Page design by Frank Corniola from the book – *Rhythm Section Drumming*

The website contains an incteractive view which highlights the different stick height whilst playing the appropriate dynamic level for the correct volume required. There is a chart and an .mp3 play along demonstrating the use of full strokes or mezzo forte stick height of 45° to begin the exercise.

Lesson 3: Counting
Introduction to Quarter Notes

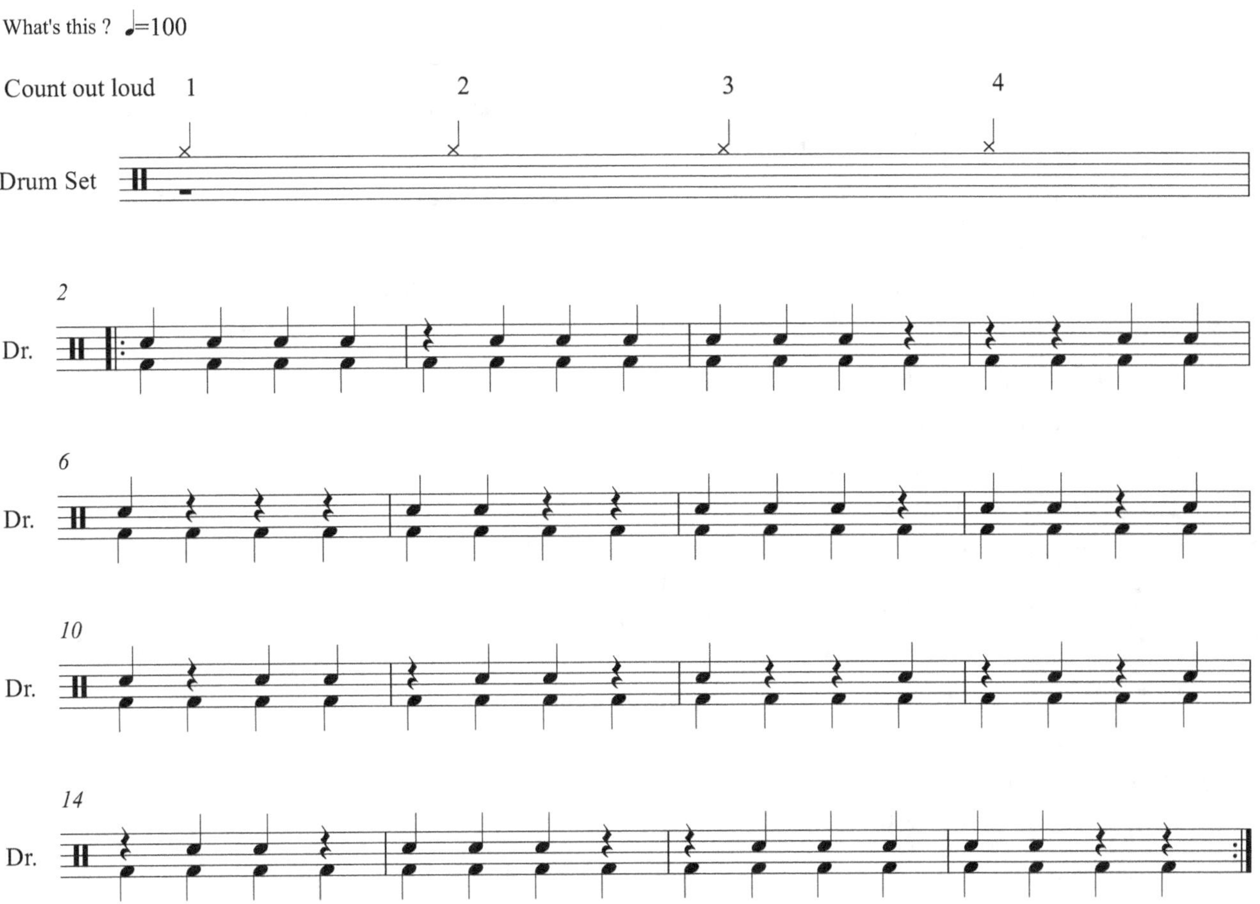

Why do we count?

Don't you find it much easier to just play as opposed to counting and playing?

That ought to tell you something about the process of counting while playing (just in case it doesn't, here's a hint: IT'S HARD!).

Usually, the things in life that take work to achieve are the things that are 'right' or 'good'. Counting while playing takes work, but it connects your limbs to your voice, which in turn connects to 'time'.

This process allows your body to connect to time in a very tangible way and lets you develop the most important attribute of all: the confidence of playing in time, with great feel.

Mike Mangini – *Rhythm Knowledge*

Lesson 3A: Tempo

Musical terms to describe slowest to fastest:

1. **Larghissimo** – very, very slow (24 BPM [beats per minute in a 4/4 time] and under)
2. **Grave** – very slow (25-45 BPM)
3. **Largo** – broadly (40-60 BPM)
4. **Lento** – slowly (45-60 BPM)
5. **Larghetto** – rather broadly (60-66 BPM)
6. **Adagio** – slow and stately (literally, "at ease") (66-76 BPM)
7. **Adagietto** – slower than andante (72- 76 BPM)
8. **Andante** – at a walking pace (76-108 BPM)
9. **Andantino** – slightly faster than andante (although in some cases it can be taken to mean slightly slower than andante) (80-108)
10. **Marcia moderato** – moderately, in the manner of a march (83-85)
11. **Andante moderato** – between andante and moderato (thus the name andante moderato) (92-122 BPM)
12. **Moderato** – moderately (108-120 BPM)
13. **Allegretto** – moderately fast (112-120 BPM)
14. **Allegretto moderato** – close but not quite allegro (116-120 BPM)
15. **Allegro** – fast, quickly, and bright (120-168 BPM) (molto allegro is slightly faster than allegro, but always in its range)
16. **Vivace** – lively and fast (168-176 BPM)
17. **Vivacissimo** – very fast and lively (172-176 BPM)
18. **Allegrissimo or Allegrovivace** – very fast (172-176 BPM)
19. **Presto** – very, very fast (168-200 BPM)
20. **Prestissimo** – even faster than presto (200 BPM and over)

Terms for tempo change:

1. **Rallentando** – gradually slowing down
2. **Ritardando** – holding back, becoming slower
3. **Ritenuto** – immediately slowing down
4. **Accelerando or Stringenda** – gradually accelerating

Lesson 4: Subdivisions

Learning Basic Notation using Sticking Subdivisions

Module Two

Coordination

**Incorporating Krupa's fifth (reading exercises)
and sixth (sticking patterns)**

Lesson 5: Relationships between hands and feet

Joe Morello states in his 1993 book *Master Studies: Everything (played on the drum kit)* is to be done with a natural body movement. You must use everything (limbs) in a natural way.

Here we begin using subdivisions with your feet. The technique is how technical details are treated, or the basic physical movements used.

The procedure I use for the feet in these exercises is "heel up". This is an advantage for my specific playing style – "activity" – which incorporates power and endurance.

The task/style is to perform Contemporary Rock Music from the past 50 years.

The following exercises are workout routines I have designed so I could practice my footwork.

It also helps me work on co-ordination, independence, and being able to concentrate on which foot is playing what grouping, while running through a rhythmic scale of even subdivisions.

It is designed to warm up your limbs (and mind). The greater the subdivision, the faster you play, all the while being disciplined by the quarter note click, which helps keep an accurate and even quality to the exercise.

This module includes Krupa's fifth (reading exercises) and sixth (sticking patterns) key methods.

Arranged by Robert Boundy
Rob's Drum Shed 2015

Lesson 5A: Relationships Worksheet

Quarter Note Foot Workout

©Robert Boundy

Lesson 6: Coordination

Basic Four-Way Coordination using Subdivisions

Lesson 6A: The 3 Basic Rudiments

Play individual Rudiment for 1 Minute Each
Beginners Tempo is MM=40 to 110
Practice all of these every day, to help build stamina, endurance and stick control.
Stick Height of *mf* = 45°

The Single Stroke Roll

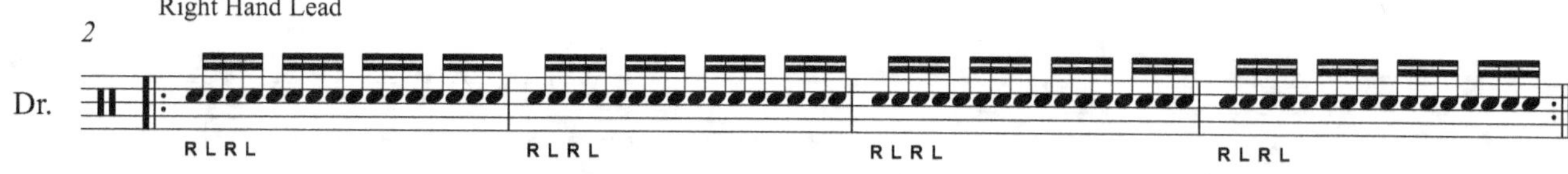

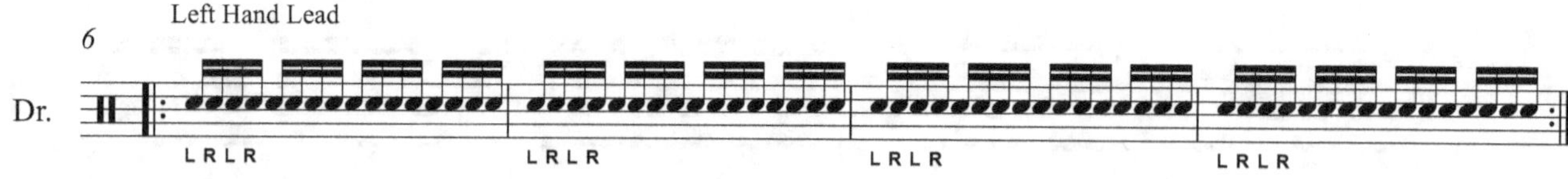

The Double Stroke Roll

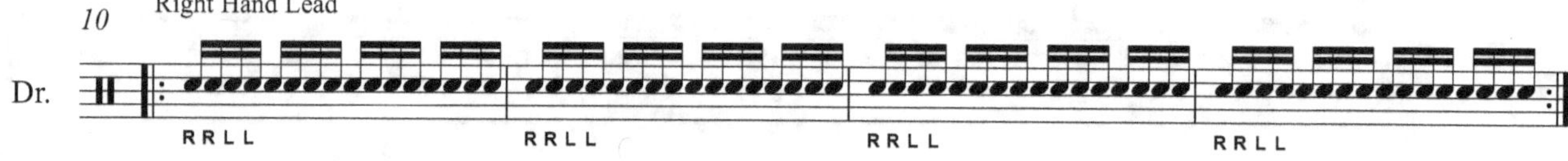

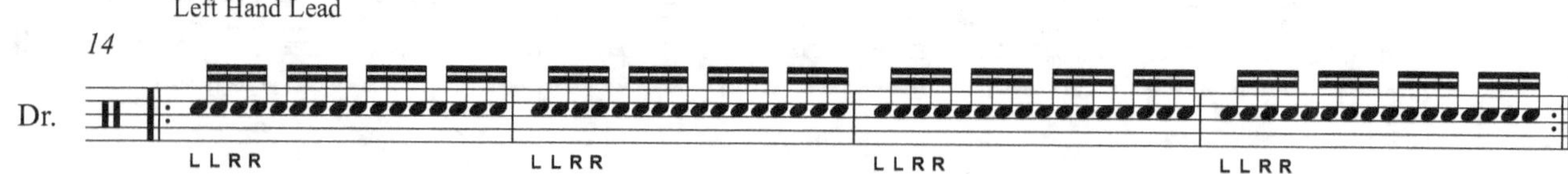

The Single Paradiddle
Accent Height is *sfz* = 90°
Non Accent Height is *mp* = 30°

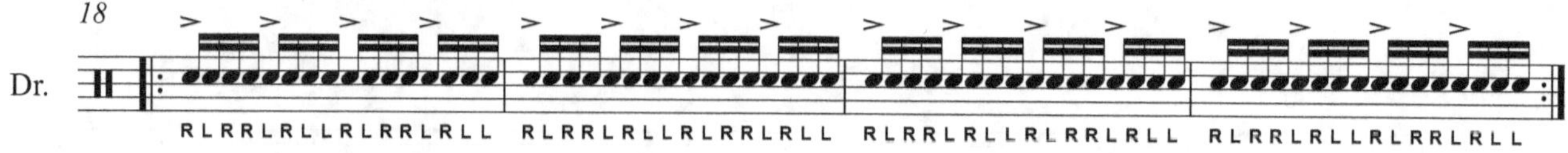

   ©Robert Boundy

Lesson 7A: 8th Notes Relationships Worksheet

Bass Drum and Hi-hat Control

Arranged by Robert Boundy
Rob's Drum Shed 2014

Lesson 7B: 8th Notes Relationships Worksheet

Double Bass Drum Control

Module Three
8th Note Rock

Incorporating Krupa's seventh (snare drum exercises), eighth (more advanced footwork) key methods.

Module Three

Incorporating Krupa's Seventh (performance pieces for snare drum), and begins the second stage of development; for the feet, the Eighth (more study of the Bass Drum/s), and Ninth (study of the Hi-hat), and then hands, Tenth (study of Hi-hat hand techniques) Key Methods

8th Note Rock begins with Lesson Eight – the creation of a musical composition using a snare drum, reading text, and adding a sound scape for a musical presentation being performed during a student's concert. The snare drum solo is called "Introducing Eighth Notes" and has been renamed "Rob's Breakfast" to add some character to the piece when performed for a concert in 2008.

As it is mostly performed by beginner level students. The metaphor of "Dog's Breakfast" can be used to describe the sound produced as loud and messy. The name was altered slightly as to be seemingly cryptic for the listener.

The piece has now been extended and developed into an accompanying drum kit chart using the basic concept of rhythms as "melodies" presented by Gary Chester's first book from 1985: The New Breed – Systems for the development of your own creativity. Chester's explanation of what he calls "systems" are designed to develop coordination, musicality, reading ability, and confidence. These also help drummers to create new and exciting material.

The system introduced in this lesson, (like Chester's "System Six") is a basic pattern played with the right hand on the Hi-hats playing eighth notes, and the left hand on the snare drum playing on beats two and four. The melody is played using the right foot on the bass drum, though not on beats two and four. Each bar is different and is to be practised individually at least four times, or as many times as it takes to get a good understanding of what you are playing. This skill learned is another of the foundational elements that develop a student's individual creativity when approaching different rhythmic and melodic scores.

Lesson 8: Snare To Drum Kit

'Rob's Breakfast'

Arranged by Robert Boundy
Rob's Drum Shed 2014

Lesson 9: 8th Note Rock Beats

Arranged by Robert Boundy
Rob's Drum Shed 2016

Lesson 10A: 8th Note Rock Beats

Summary Page 1

Part I 'Stereo Alien'

Arranged by Robert Boundy
Rob's Drum Shed 2016

Lesson 10A: 8th Note Rock Beats

Part I 'Fishing with Riley'

Part II 'Leave him at the Bus stop'

Arranged by Robert Boundy
Rob's Drum Shed 2016

Lesson 10+ Bonus

'A Day at The Beach'

Module Four
8th Note Rests

Incorporating Krupa's ninth (introduction to hands playing Hi-hats) key method.

Module Four

Lesson Eleven, *8th Note Rests*, carries on the
compositional theme for performance pieces using
the Chester concepts once again.

The chart/workbook is titled *"Rob's Morning Tea"*,
continuing with the theme presented earlier, moving
forward through the course.

There are now four examples presented within this
lesson:

1. The online video clip has the music score
   embedded at the bottom, allowing students
   to follow along with the demonstration
   of the drum kit piece (played with the
   backing track) to be learnt in this lesson.
2. There is also a video clip demonstrating
   the snare drum solo played along
   with the music score.
3. The .pdf of the complete lesson is available
   to download, as with all lessons.
4. There is an .mp3 of the backing track without
   drums, for the student to play along to. This
   can be downloaded and saved on the student's
   preferred device.

The introduction to fills and open Hi-hat techniques
are covered within this lesson to prepare students
for the upcoming combination studies.

Transcribed by Robert Boundy
Rob's Drum Shed 2012

Lesson 11: 8th Note Rests

'Rob's Morning Tea'

30

Lesson 11A: Rock Beats Page 1

12 bar summary with fills and Open Hi Hats

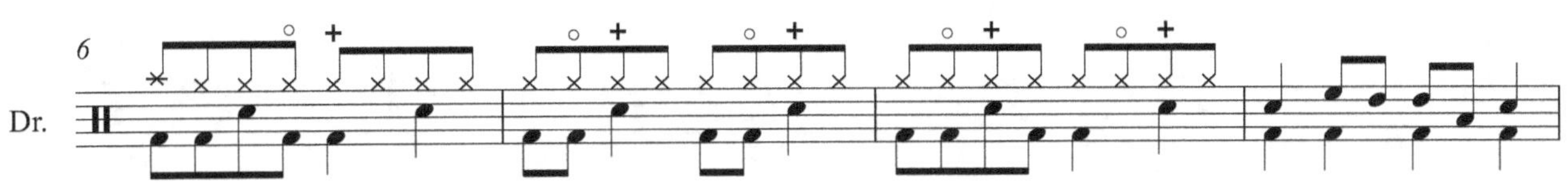

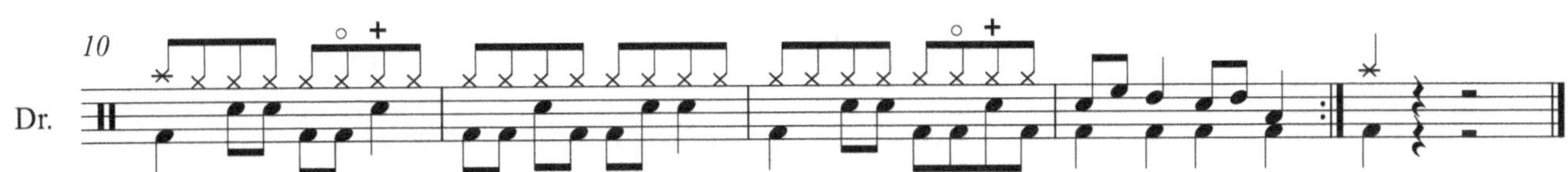

Lesson 12: 8th Note Syncopation

Part I Combination Exercise

Part II 'Jigsaw'

©Robert Boundy

Lesson 13: 8th Note Rests

Four-Bar Patterns Combining Two-Bar Patterns

Lesson 14: Rock Beats
8th Note Rock Beats with Rests

This lesson introduces rudimental elements (Krupa's Sixth Key Method) that dynamically embellish the performance.

Starting with the introduction of flams consisting of two strokes that are dynamically different and played slightly apart from each other to thicken the sound of the beat played.

The notes are played with an element of syncopation in the opening bar, voiced between hands and feet.

Transcribed by Robert Boundy
Rob's Drum Shed 2016

Module Five

Hi-Hat Work

Advancing Krupa's ninth and tenth (Open Hi-hat techniques, Bass Drum techniques, and drum fills) key methods

Module Five

Hi-hat work contains lessons that explore the left foot and right hand operating and playing the Hi-hat cymbals, exploring various approaches, beginning with:

1. Lesson Fifteen – open Hi-hat work uses Jackson's examples developed into eight two-bar rhythms to play through, then repeated for a total of thirty-two bars.
2. There is a one-bar Hi-hat break pattern which sets up the next combination of four two-bar exercises as an eight-bar section that is repeated.

Combination Summary: this lesson refers to lesson fourteen, developing eighth note fills, introducing sixteenth note fills, incorporating open Hi-hat work and rudiments, combining those elements, and helping to review your musical knowledge.

Arranged by Robert Boundy
Rob's Drum Shed 2016

Lesson 15: Open Hi-hat Work

'Rock Beats'

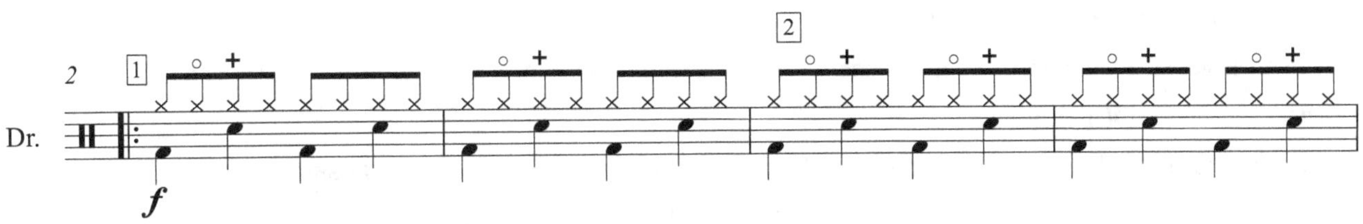

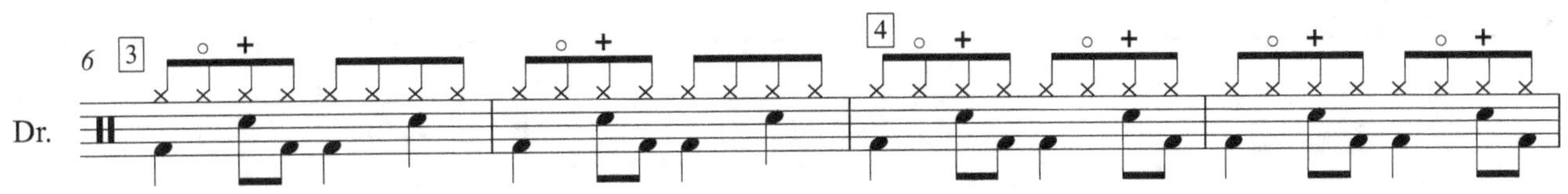

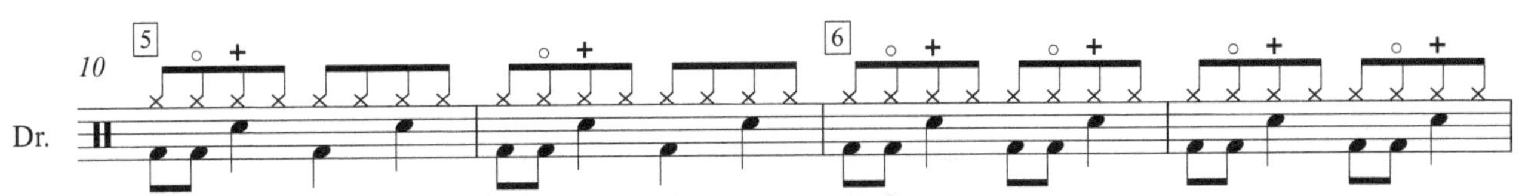

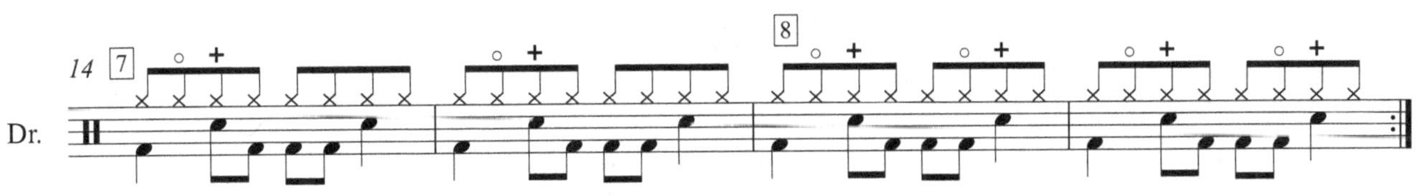

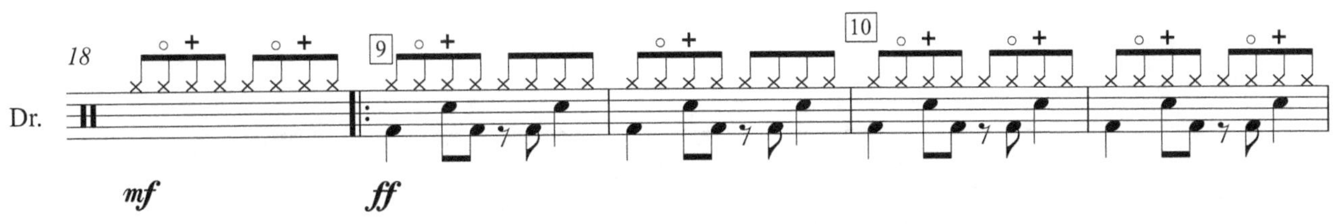

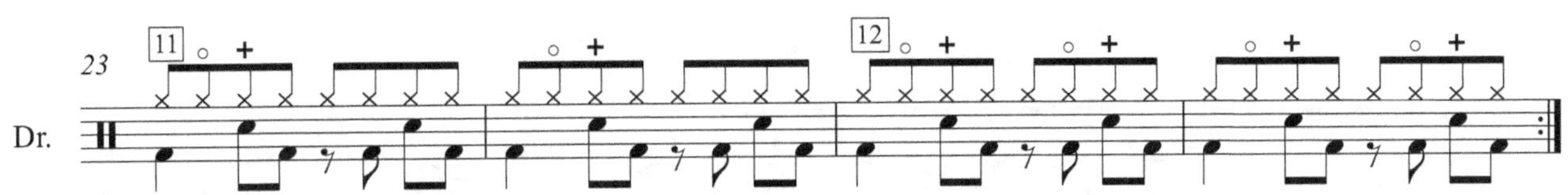

Lesson 16: Combination Summary

'Redneck'

This chart introduces a different musical genre for this backing track.

The website play-along was created using a sample of Heavy Metal Band "Lamb of God's" track *Redneck* [1] from a play along track taken from Educational Drum set publication Rhythm. [2]

The track is slowed and demonstrates how to use foundation-level drumming elements to perform in the style of groove metal.

[1] CJ Adler, DR Blythe, MD Morton and JS Campbell, Redneck, Subtle Arts Publishing, Sony/ATV Publishing.Faber Music. Reproduced by permission of Hal Leonard Corporation. 2006. CD

[2] Mike Sturgis, Rhythm Drum Lessons- Rhythm Drum Magazine Issue 154, Somerset, Future Publishing, 2008. 80

Arranged by Robert Boundy
Rob's Drum Shed 2017 - Arranged and Edited

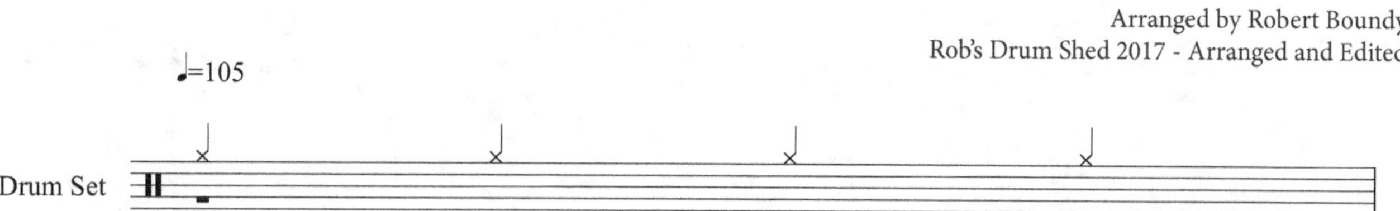

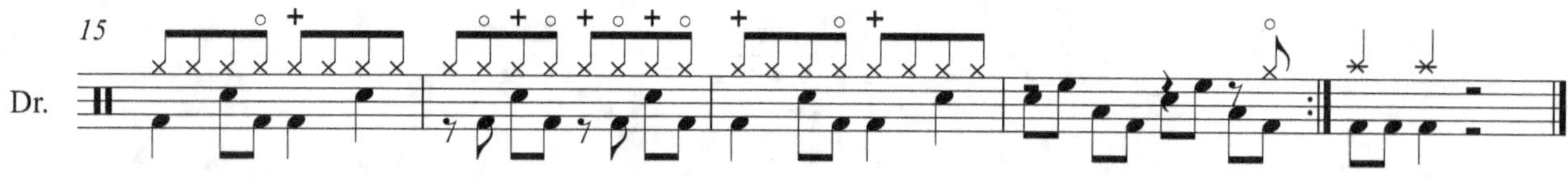

Lesson 17: Note Groupings

Note groupings introduces playing groups of two bass drum notes that begin every three Hi-hat notes, creating a basic polyrhythm using eighth note rhythms.

This exercise is in 4/4 time, so the bass drumbeat comes back to the beginning every three bars. The next two exercises are then displaced by a single eighth note shifting the feel of the pulse of the rhythm.

This concept was inspired by having some small part in the creation of Virgil Donati's 1989 video release *Obsessive Rhythms* (I was working at Drumworld in Melbourne at the time). In more recent times, whilst exploring Gavin Harrison's rhythmic displacement ideas from his book *Rhythmic Illusions*, I decided this was a simpler approach to introduce how to understand a polyrhythm, i.e. playing two or more rhythms at the same time, not readily perceived as deriving from one another.

This lesson will aid you in beginning to understand more developed rhythmic concepts, as these rhythms have been broken down for the foundation level course.

Cont.

Arranged by Robert Boundy
Rob's Drum Shed 2016

Lesson 17: Note groupings

Module Six
Summary

Krupa's fourteenth key method, playing along with popular songs

RDS Lesson 18

'The Thing'

Module Six –The final module of The Foundation Series of lessons incorporates Krupa's Fourteenth key method.

The final stage at a basic level for student development: playing along with published music of popular songs.

©S Williamson, C Farley, M Lodge, R Boundy - Laneway Music 2019

RDS - Lesson 19

Quarter Note Rock Summary

INTERMEDIATE SYLLABUS

Intermediate Syllabus

The next section of this book is the Intermediate syllabus. This section takes the student through more advanced lessons and song transcriptions.

Krupa's Fourteenth key method could be viewed as the 'final' stage of a student's development. The more advanced charts and transcriptions towards the end of this section are from my own personal published compositions from recorded performances with my band, the Virgin Soldiers (we still perform currently through 2019 and 2020, actively writing and releasing new material).

Though these songs were written and performed during the mid- to late-80s and early 90s, I transcribed my parts in as much detail as possible; the discipline is in the attention to detail of these parts and honouring my original ideas (I am still forever working on improving how I play them).

I encourage all my intermediate level students to begin to write out their musical ideas as it gives you a deeper understanding of music from a more technical level. This stage of development is designed as an aid to improve your aural skills which will assist you in understanding the musical arrangements and song structure.

I hope it helps you grow as a musician and constantly challenge you to stay inspired and motivated with your own practice.

Module One
Triplets

Lesson 1

'Rob's Lunch'

Lesson 1A: Relationships

Introduction to Bass Drum Control - Triplets

Drum Set

All Left Foot patterns can be played with HiHat if you don't have a left foot Bass Drum/Pedal.
Each line can be played in dividually at first.

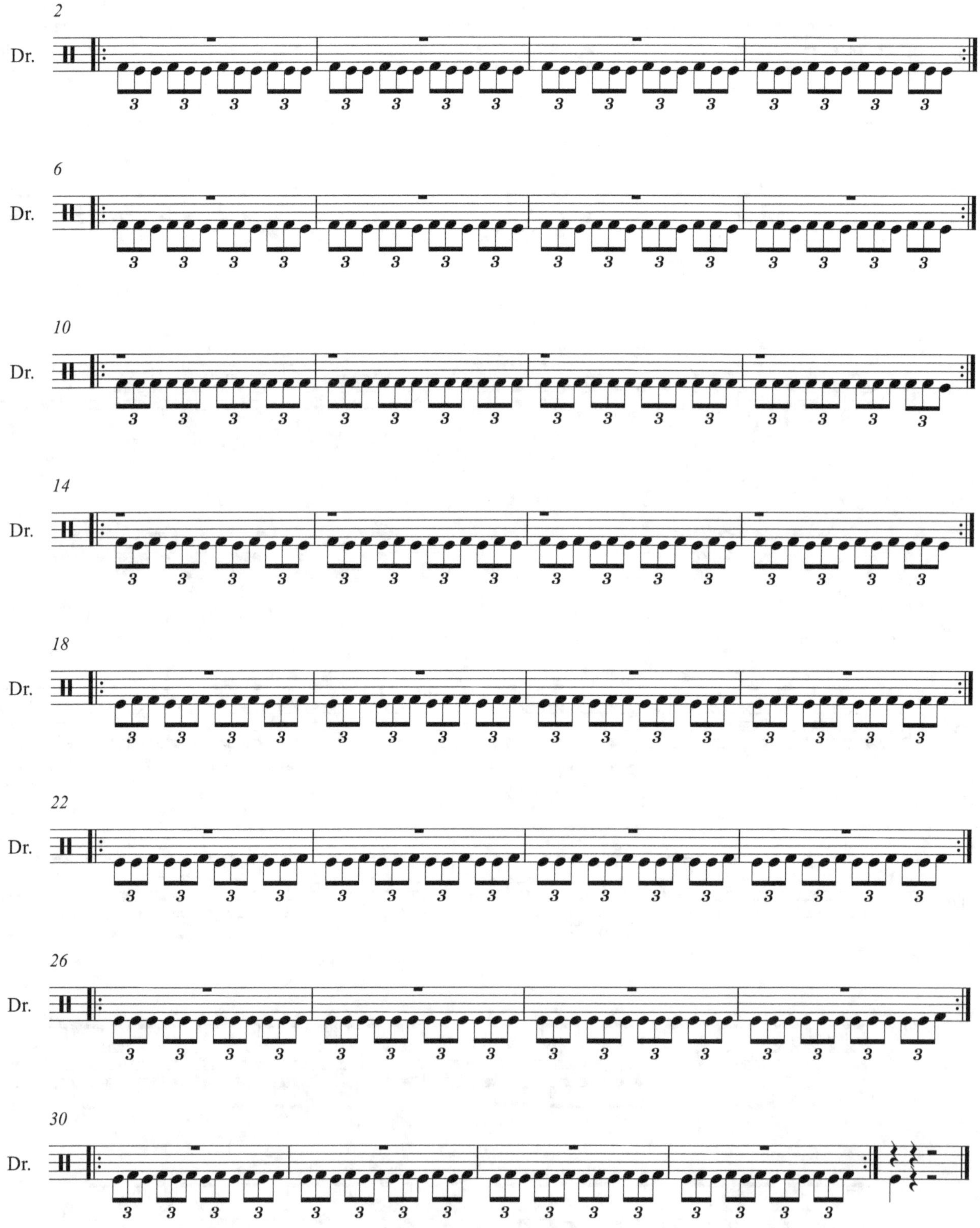

©Robert Boundy

Lesson 2: 8th Note Triplet Rests

Shuffles

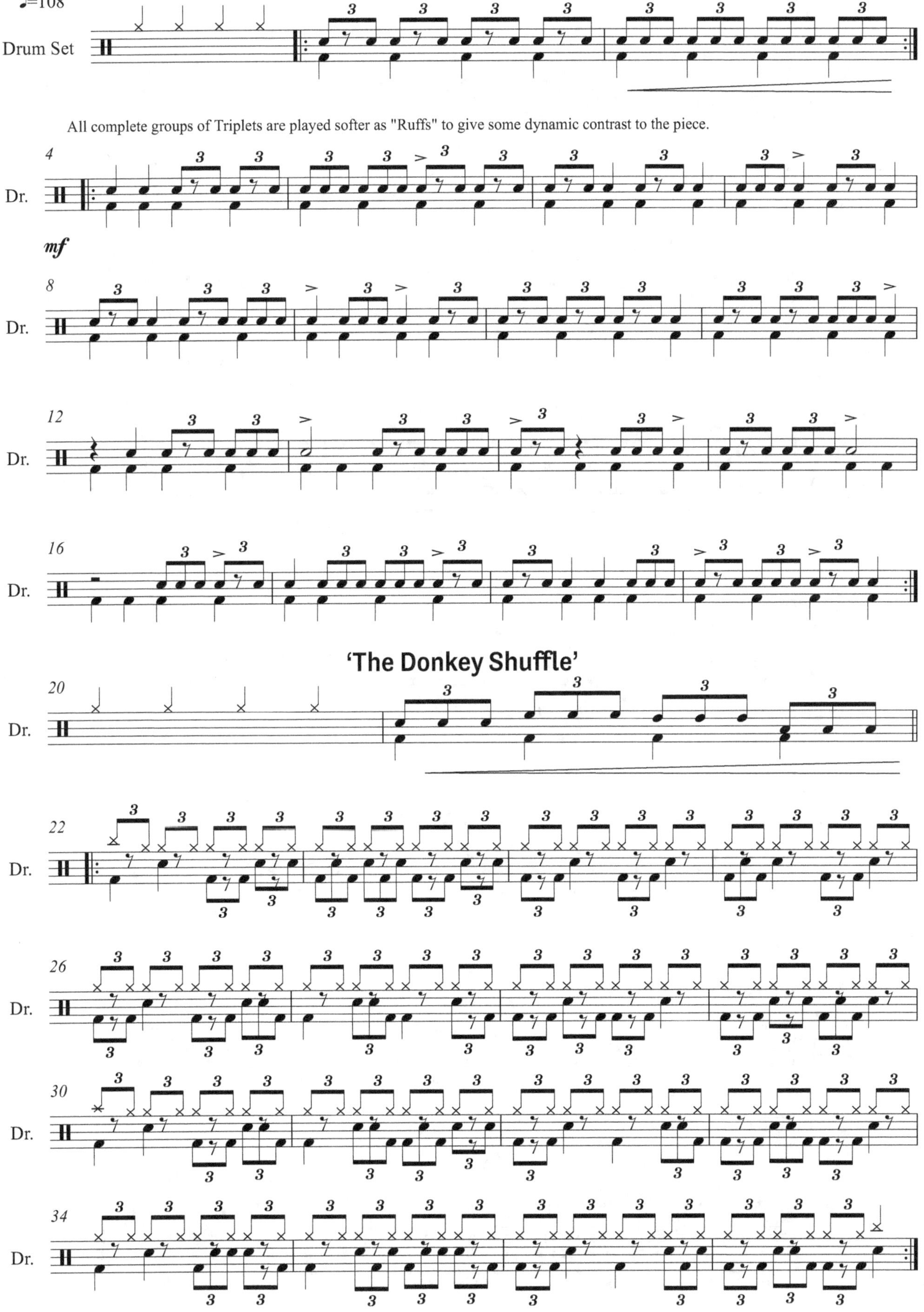

Lesson 2A: Shuffle Patterns with Fills

'The Rosie Shuffle'

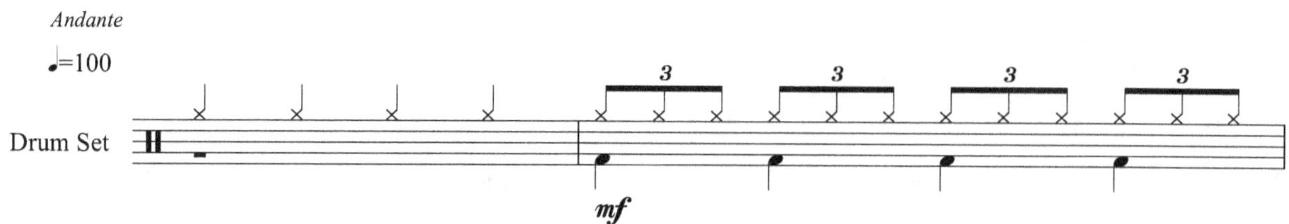

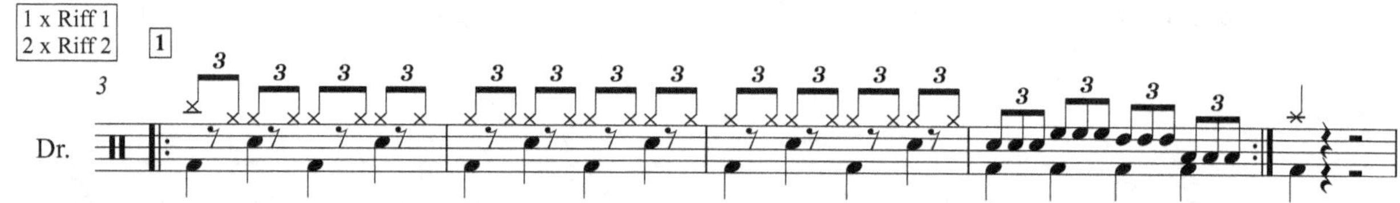

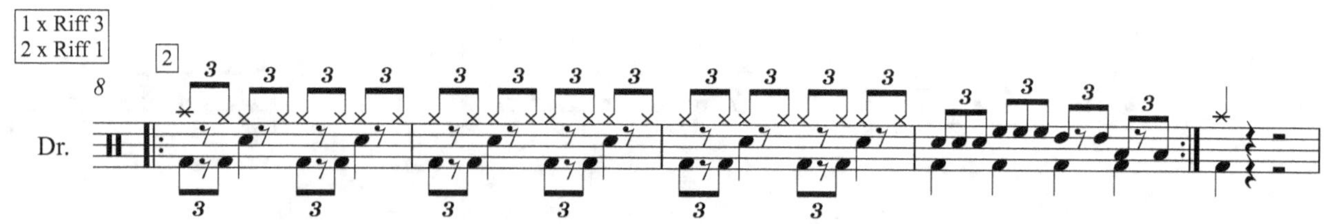

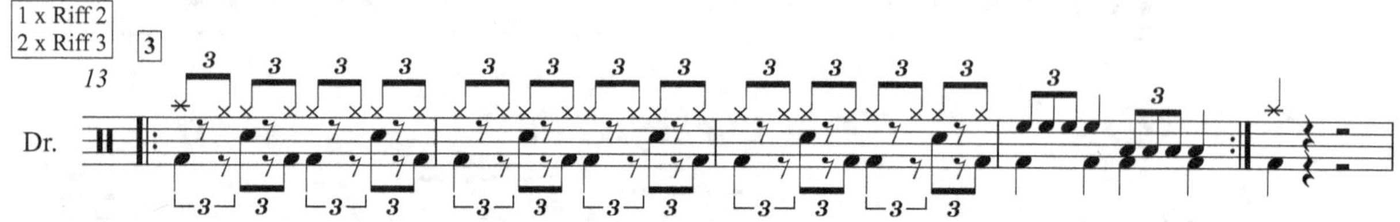

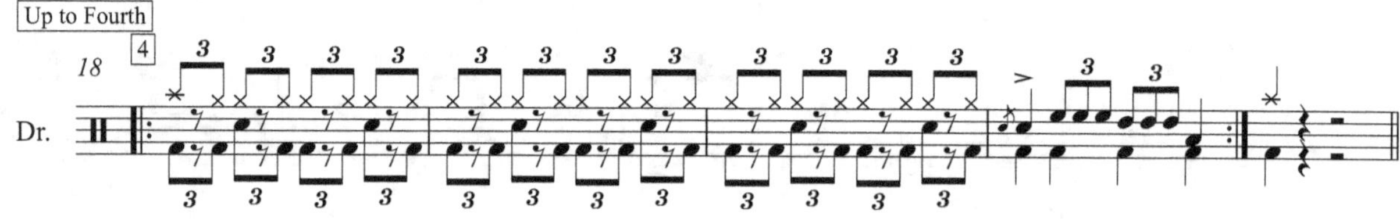

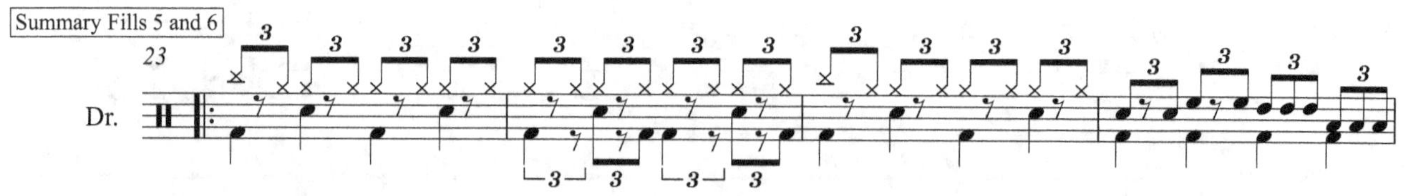

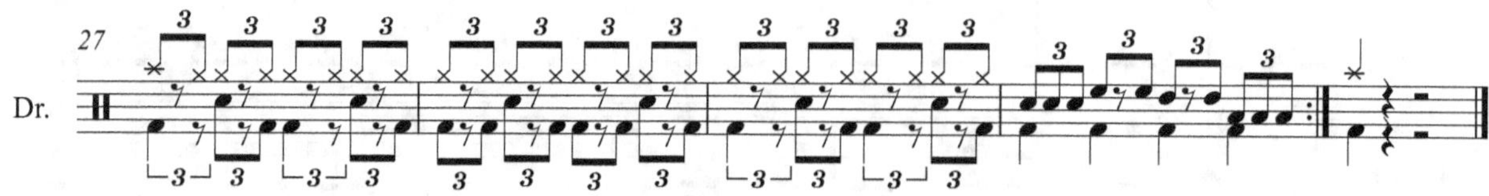

©Robert Boundy

Module Two
Sixteenth Notes

Lesson 3: 16th Notes with dynamics

'The Bugsy March'

Including Accents and Dynamics

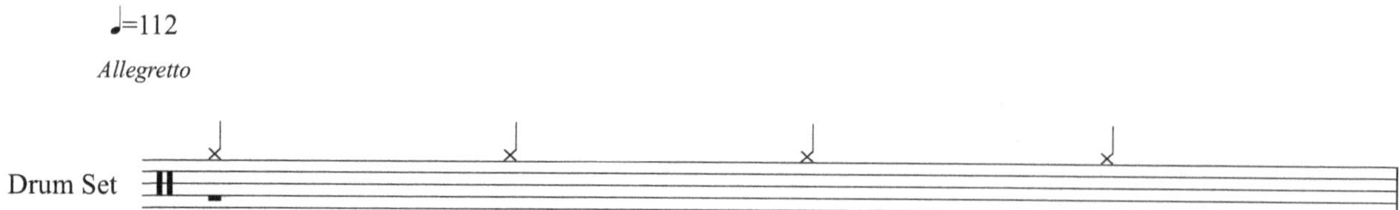

Use alternating sticking, pay attention to dynamics.

This is a good snare drum piece to practice your marching skills too.
Remember to start on your left foot !

Beat 1 -Left Foot, Beat 2 - Right Foot, Beat 3-Left Foot, Beat 4 -Right Foot, ect.

Lesson 4: 16ths and 8ths

'Rob's Afternoon Tea'

Including Accents and Dynamics

Arranged by Robert Boundy
Rob's Drum Shed 2016

Lesson 5: 16th Note Rock Beats

'Monster'

This chart features text guides to the arrangement of the song.
Note, Groove Section, Vox (Vocals Section),Chorus

©Ryu Sang-Gu, SM Entertainment

Module Three
Accents

Lesson 6: Accented 16th notes

Page 1

©Robert Boundy

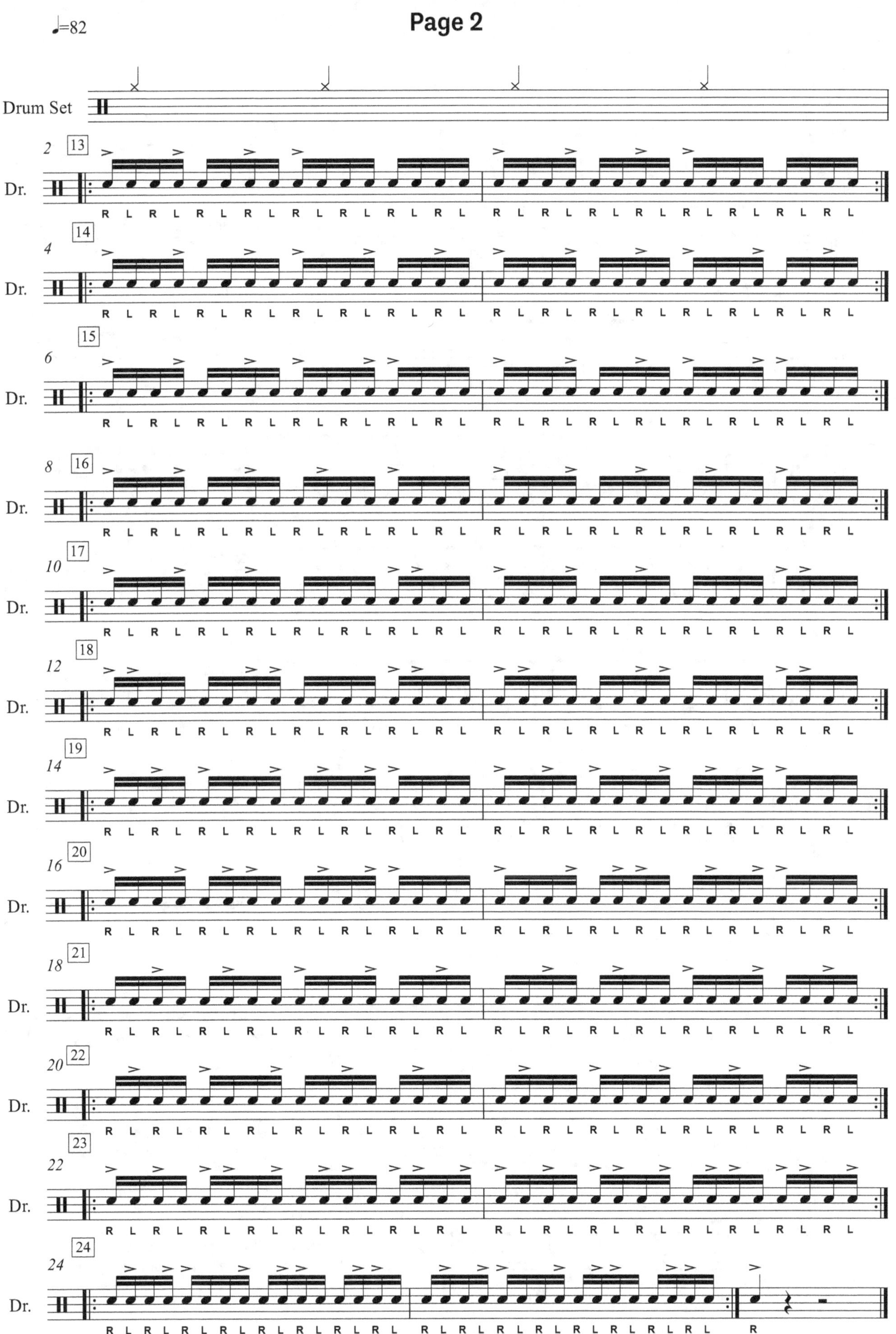Arranged by Robert Boundy
Rob's Drum Shed 2012
Lesson 6A: Accented 16th notes
Page 2
♩=82
Drum Set
2 13
Dr.
R L R L R L R L R L R L R L R L   R L R L R L R L R L R L R L R L
4 14
Dr.
R L R L R L R L R L R L R L R L   R L R L R L R L R L R L R L R L
6 15
Dr.
R L R L R L R L R L R L R L R L   R L R L R L R L R L R L R L R L
8 16
Dr.
R L R L R L R L R L R L R L R L   R L R L R L R L R L R L R L R L
10 17
Dr.
R L R L R L R L R L R L R L R L   R L R L R L R L R L R L R L R L
12 18
Dr.
R L R L R L R L R L R L R L R L   R L R L R L R L R L R L R L R L
14 19
Dr.
R L R L R L R L R L R L R L R L   R L R L R L R L R L R L R L R L
16 20
Dr.
R L R L R L R L R L R L R L R L   R L R L R L R L R L R L R L R L
18 21
Dr.
R L R L R L R L R L R L R L R L   R L R L R L R L R L R L R L R L
20 22
Dr.
R L R L R L R L R L R L R L R L   R L R L R L R L R L R L R L R L
22 23
Dr.
R L R L R L R L R L R L R L R L   R L R L R L R L R L R L R L R L
24 24
Dr.
R L R L R L R L R L R L R L R L   R L R L R L R L R L R L R L R L   R
©Robert Boundy
57

Lesson 7: Accented 16th Note Fills

©Robert Boundy

Arranged by Robert Boundy
Rob's Drum Shed 2015

Lesson 8: Alternating 16th Note Patterns

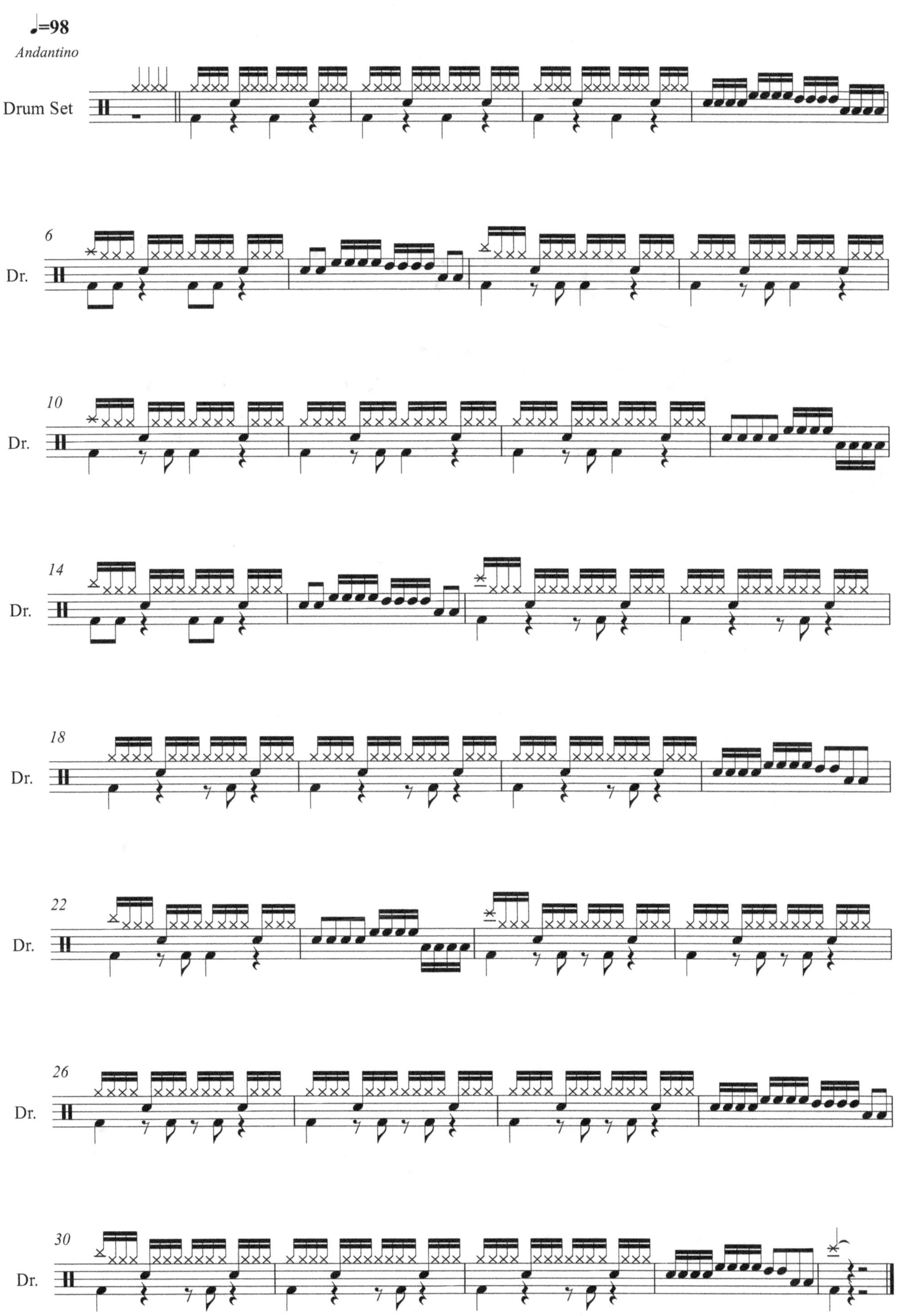

Module Four
Triplets and Subdivisions

Arranged by Robert Boundy
Rob's Drum Shed 2012

Lesson 9: Basic Triplet Notation using Sticking Subdivions

Arranged by Robert Boundy
Rob's Drum Shed 2012

Lesson 10: Double Bass Drums 16th Note Subdivision

Lesson 11: Dotted Notes

Lesson 12: 8th Note Triplet Accents

Page 1

©Robert Boundy

Lesson 12A: 8th Note Triplet Accents

Page 2

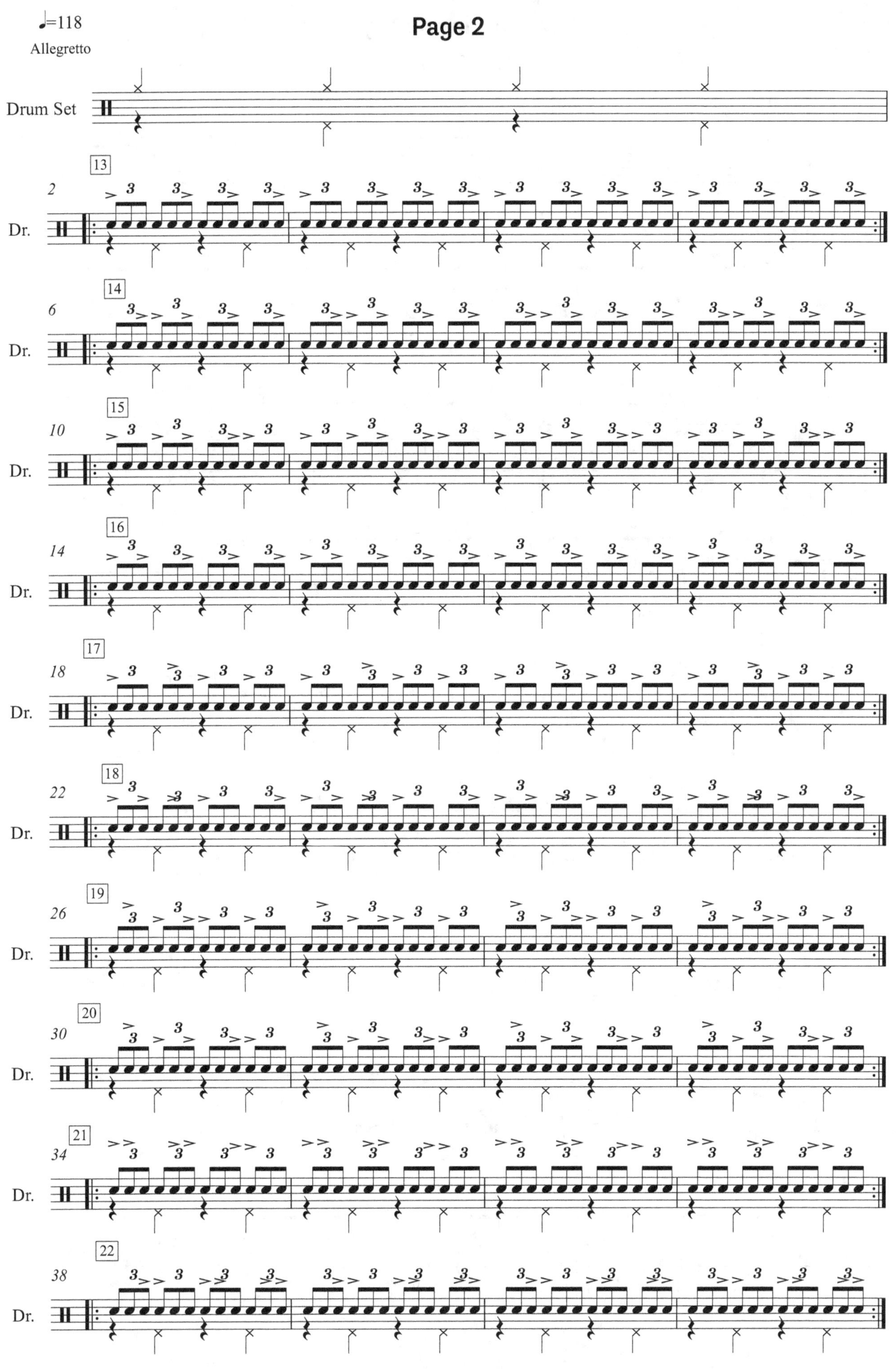

Transcribed by Robert Boundy 2021

Lesson 12: Summary

'Danger in The Night'

from the EP 'Virgin Soldiers'

♩=124

Composed and arranged by Farley, Williamson,
Boundy, Lodge, Marquis 1987

©S Williamson, C Farley, M Lodge, R Boundy, G Marquis - Soldier Records 1987

Dr.
Guitar Solo
Dr.
Dr.
Dr.
Pre Chorus
Dr.
Chorus
Dr.
Dr.
Dr.
Dr.
Dr.
88
92
96
100
104
109
112
115
117
119
ff
ff
ff
ff

Module Five
Grooves and Combinations

Arranged by Robert Boundy
Rob's Drum Shed 2017

Lesson 13: 16th Note Grooves Sheet

Arranged by Robert Boundy
Rob's Drum Shed 2017

Lesson 14: Accented Grooves

©Robert Boundy

Arranged by Robert Boundy
Rob's Drum Shed 2017

Lesson 15: 16th Note Combination 1

Lesson 16: 16th Note Combination 2

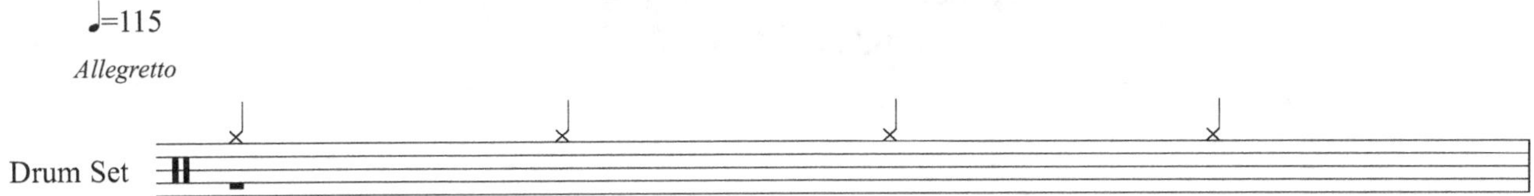

'Boompa Zoonka'

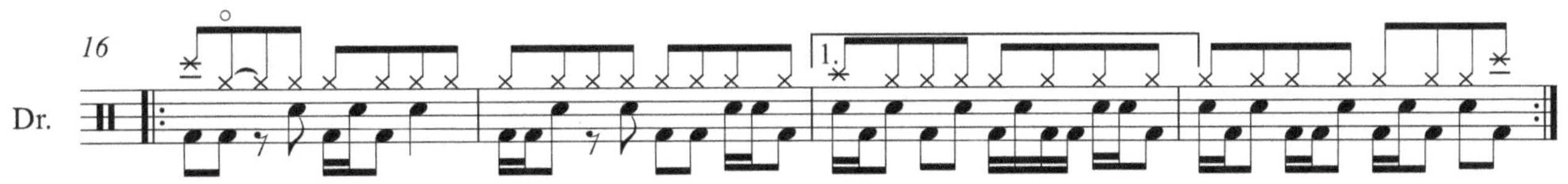

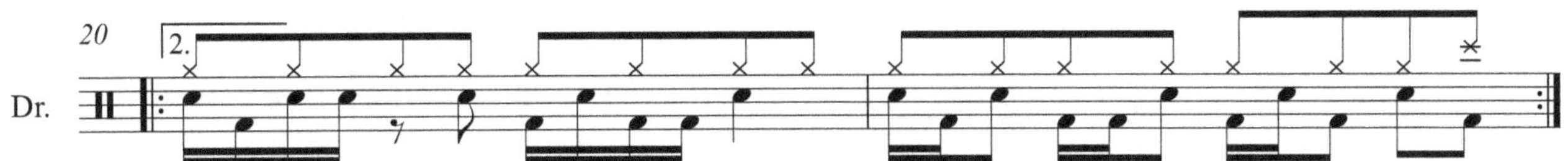

Arranged by Robert Boundy
Rob's Drum Shed 2017

Lesson 17: 16th Note Combination 3

'Odd Robert'

'Bobby Bizarro'

Module Six

Summary

Arranged by Robert Boundy
Rob's Drum Shed 2017

Lesson 18: Mixing 16th Note Combinations

'Soup before Dinner'

Lesson 19: 16 Note Combinations

'Carmine's Grooves'

This chart is inspired by one of my favourite rock drummers Carmine Appice. I discovered his book in 1979 and it was a turning point in my study of the instrument.

Check out Carmine's playing with Vanilla Fudge, Jeff Beck and Rod Stewart from that era. I was heavily influenced by his playing and as it is a great example of how to use 16th note combinations. His book *Realistic Rock Drumming* deserves a place in your drum book collection. The play-along on the Rob's Drum Shed website is especially written for this great groove. Remember to be musical in your approach to all these charts!

Arranged by Robert Boundy
Rob's Drum Shed 2017

Lesson 20: 16th Note Bass Drum Combinations w/fills

'Rob's Dinner'

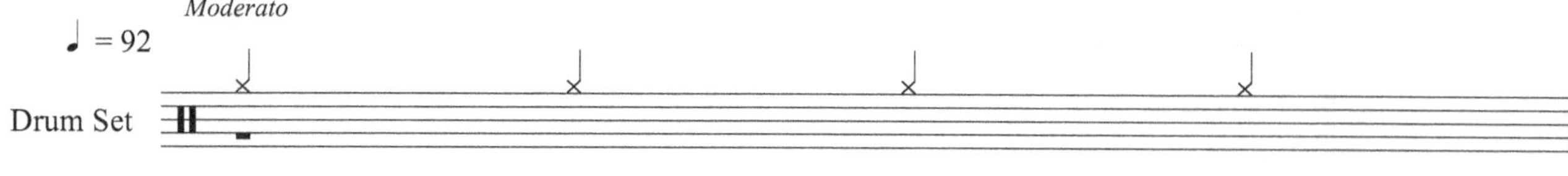

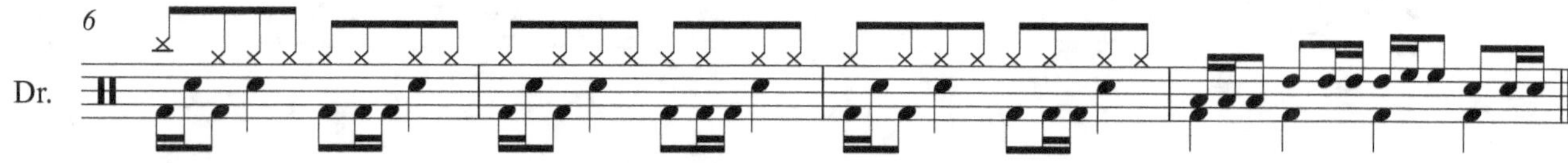

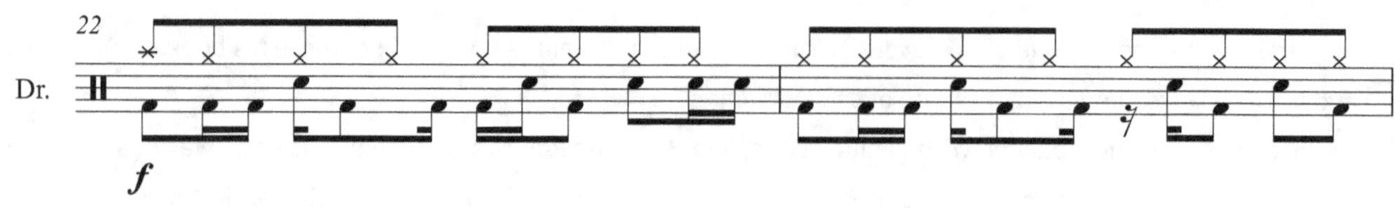

Written by Virgin Soldiers
Arranged 2019 Transcribed by Robert Boundy

Lesson 20A

'Junkies Paradise'

Written by Virgin Soldiers
Arranged 2019 Transcribed by Robert Boundy

Verse 2
Dr.
mf
Dr.
Dr.
1.
2.
Chorus
Dr.
Dr.
Chorus Repeat
Dr.
Riff
Dr.
Dr.
3
3
Dr.
3
Guitar Solo
Dr.
Dr.
Chorus Repeat
Dr.
Dr.

Written by Virgin Soldiers
Arranged 2019 Transcribed by Robert Boundy

111
Dr.
1.
2.
+ Verse 3
115
Dr.
+
1.
2.
119
Chorus
Dr.
123
Dr.
127
Chorus Repeat
Dr.
Riff
131
Dr.
135
Chorus
Dr.
Outro
139
Dr.
143
Dr.

Arranged by Robert Boundy
Rob's Drum Shed 2012

Lesson 21: 16th Note Combinations Summary

'Go four a wander'

Drum Set

©Robert Boundy

Written by Virgin Soldiers 1988
Transcribed by Robert Boundy

Lesson 22: Summary

'Breaking Loose'

From the Album 'Watching The World'

46
Dr.
49
Dr.
52
Dr.
55
Dr.
58
Dr.
Verse 3
61
Dr.
65
Dr.
Chorus III
69
Dr.
73
Dr.
77
Dr.
80
1.
2.
Dr.
83
rit.
Dr.

Lesson 23: Summary

'Never Too Late'

(Never Too Late, page 2)

©S Williamson, C Farley, M Lodge, R Boundy, G Marquis - Soldier Records 1990

(Never Too Late, page 3)

These songs I wrote, arranged, and transcribed are from my band 'Virgin Soldiers'.

They are great examples of combinations of all the previous lesson note groupings (and a few more).

Double Bass Drum Grooves, featuring combinations of note values, exciting fills, grace notes, dynamics, and all the subtleties and inflections you can use to create your own drum parts.

The art is in the learning and understanding how they all fit together to make music.

Good luck on the journey, and I do hope you get to learn something from the examples in this book.

-Rob

Written by Virgin Soldiers 1989
Transcribed by Robert Boundy

Lesson 24: Summary

'Hell Night - Introduction'

From the Album 'Watching The World'

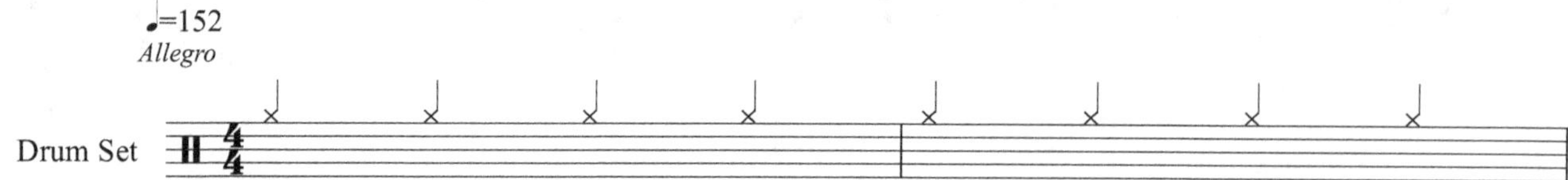

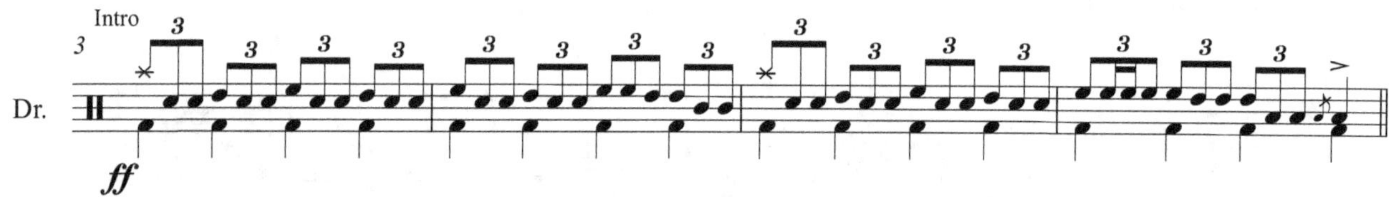

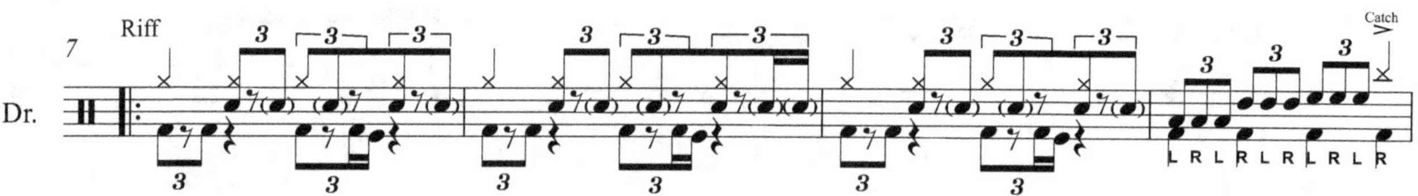

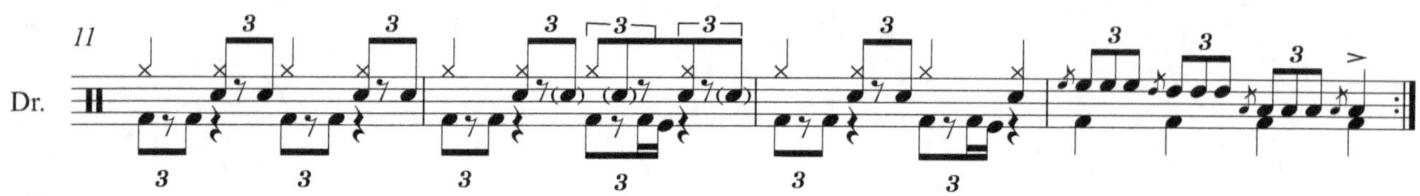

RDS Intermediate Lesson 25
Rhythm Scale

HiHat Left Foot Plays on Beats 2 and 4
Bass Drum Right Foot Plays 4 to the Bar

Right Hand Lead

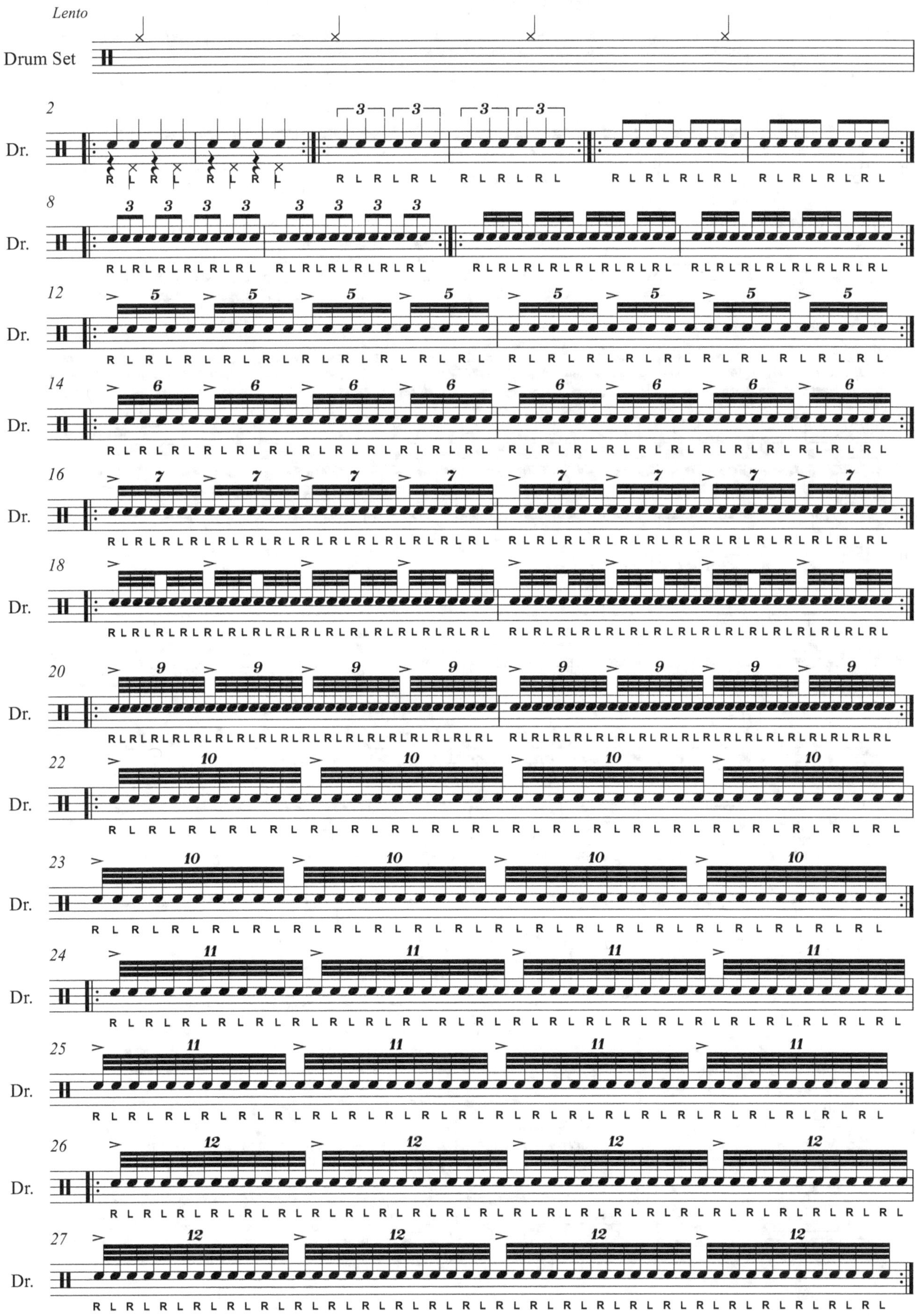

$\quarternote=53$

Lento

Transcribed by Robert Boundy
Written by Virgin Soldiers 1986

Lesson 26

'Make a Change'

From the Album 'Virgin Soldiers Live 2019'

2

References

Appice, C. (1972). *The updated Realistic Rock Drum Method.* Beverly Hills: Alfreds.
Atkinson, M. (2003). *The Unreel Drum Book.* Miami: Warner Brother Publications.

Australian Music Examinations Board. (1998). *CPM Drum Kit Steps 1- 4 Advancing.* Melbourne: AMEB.

Boundy, R. (2013). Website *Rob's Drum Shed-Foundations*. RDS Productions.

Chester, G. (1985). *The New Breed-Systems for the development of your own creativity.* Cedar Grove NJ: Modern Drummer Publications.

CJ Adler, D. B. (2006). Redneck [Recorded by Lamb of God]. *On Sacrament* [CD]. Virginia.

Corniola, F. (1985). *Rhythm Section Drumming.* Melbourne: Musictek.

Dahlgren and Fine, M. D. (1963). 4 -Way Coordination _ A method Book for Complete Independance on the DRUM SET. New York: Belwin Mills Publishing Corp.

Donati, V. (1989). *Obsessive Rhythms.* Melbourne: DBD Production.

Famularo, D. (1999). *It's Your Move- Motions and Emotions.* Coram N.Y.: Wizdom Enterprises.

Harrison, G. (1996). *Rhythmic Illusions.* Florida: Warner Music Publications. Jackson, T. (2015). *The Complete Drummer's Guide.* Melbourne: DTB Publications. Krupa, G. (1938). *Drum Method.* New York: Robbins Music Coorporation.

Mangini, M. (1997). *Rhythm Knowledge (Vol. 1).* Canada: Rhythm Knowledge.

Reed, T. (1958). *Progressive Steps to Syncopation for the Modern Drummer.* Van Nuys CA: Alfred Publishing Company.

Stone, G. L. (1935) *Stick Control,* Massachusetts: Alfred Music

Zero G.(2016). *Vinyl Classics.* Ableton Live 9 Packs. Ableton.

Acknowledgements

I would like to thank my wife, Michelle, for the inspiration, love, and support throughout my career as a musician, and for sharing our journey together in music as teachers and creative artists.

To musician, website designer, and friend, Peter Donovan, for making the dream of my teaching website come alive. Sound engineer and friend, the late Malcolm Hay from Guessongs Studios, for sharing your professionalism, workspace, talent, and objectivity.

To my drum teachers, Larry Todd, Lindsay Chuck, Frank Corniola, Jeff Barnes, Laurie Kennedy, Greg Bassani OAM, Craig Lauritsen, and the Australian Drumming Community, thank you for the opportunities and inspiration.

My mentor and friend, Steve Todd, ex-South Australian Police Band and ex-Director of the Raiders Drum Corp.

To Tom Jackson and Virgil Donati for your inspiration, generosity, and passion for percussion education.

To Professor Aaron Corn, Dr Luke Harrald, and Dr Emily Dollman from The University of Adelaide, and Mrs Pamela Charles for your constant support, advice, and guidance.

To Kosta Perkas, Jerry Tsitas, Jack Thomson, and Harry Freeman from Derringers Drum Shop SA, thanks for keeping it real.

To Lea Rose from Tattoo Rose Promotions, Chris Farley, Stephen Williamson, Mick Lodge, and Ron Marsden from The Virgin Soldiers, thanks for keeping the musical dream alive.

Front cover photo taken by Veronica Ellis, and used with kind permission.

Back cover photo taken by photographer Lea Rose, and used with kind permission.

Robs Drum Shed Productions - 2022

Boundy, Robert (author)

Foundations:
A Workbook to Develop Practice Skills and Knowledge for Playing the Drum Kit

979-0-9022687-2-1
MUSIC / Drum
Tenso 10/15
Cover and book design by Green Hill Publishing

https://robsdrumshed.com